Epinician Odes and
Dithyrambs of Bacchylides

Epinician Odes and Dithyrambs of Bacchylides

Translated by David R. Slavitt

PENN

University of Pennsylvania Press

Philadelphia

Copyright © 1998 University of Pennsylvania Press
All rights reserved
Printed in the United States of America on acid-free paper

10 9 8 7 6 5 4 3 2 1

Published by
University of Pennsylvania Press
Philadelphia, Pennsylvania 19104-4011

Library of Congress Cataloging-in-Publication Data
Bacchylides.
   [Works. English]
   Epinician odes and dithyrambs of Bacchylides / translated by
David R. Slavitt.
      p.   cm.
   ISBN 0-8122-3447-2 (cloth : alk. paper)
   1. Bacchylides—Translations into English.   2. Laudatory poetry,
Greek—Translations into English.   3. Odes—Translations into
English.   4. Athletics—Greece—Poetry.   5. Games—Greece—
Poetry.   I. Slavitt, David R., 1935–   .   II. Title.
PA3943.E5   1998b
884′.01—dc21   97-50450
                                                           CIP

For Greta and Bob
May the god never tire of doing you good.
Beside the swirling Alpheus, golden Dawn
looked down to see Pherenicus' chestnut mane
and the victory of your horse,
running with the speed of an oncoming storm . . .
                                         —Ode V

Contents

Introduction   I

Epinician Odes   9

Dithyrambs   65

Introduction

Bacchylides, if he is known at all to the general reader, is a kind of Boccherini to Pindar's Haydn, an also-ran. Pindar, Robert Fagles said in his version of Bacchylides' poems of more than thirty years ago,[1] "is by far the greater poet," although he does go on to admit that "To blame Bacchylides for not being Pindar is as childish a judgment as to condemn . . . Marvell for missing the grandeur of Milton."

I like underdogs. I am also an admirer of modest excellence. Milton is not a poet I read for pleasure, or, indeed, much at all these days, while I do look at Marvell from time to time. And this is not because I am so determined an eccentric. On the contrary, I'd claim that my judgment is the normative one, the reaction of

---

1. *Bacchylides: Complete Poems* (New Haven, Conn.: Yale University Press, 1961).

an amateur who is not a part of the academic establishment and whose views, therefore, are not much influenced by which poets lend themselves to pedagogical exercises. Nobody runs courses in Herrick, but that doesn't mean Herrick isn't a great poet. Indeed, he is so good that there is almost nothing to say about his work. The elegance and the accomplishment of each piece is all but self-evident, and analysis, though possible, seems otiose and absurd.

The need to explicate or to provide students with material that can be grist for their intellectual mill is, at the very least, a distortion of the poetic topography. Bacchylides deserves attention not because he is beetling, like Pindar, but because he is not. He relies on craftsmanship and reliably displays an attractive grace and elegance. The English poet he most resembles, I think, is neither Herrick nor Marvell but Dryden, who is probably the paradigmatic dead white European male. (He is at any rate one of the first to be thrown to those equal-opportunity feminist and ethnic wolves baying just behind the departmental droshkies.)

These were reasons enough for me to take a look at Bacchylides. There was a further reward, too, in that, whenever strangers at parties asked me what I was working on (as they often do, perhaps supposing they are doing me a favor by pretending to be interested) I was able for a time to reply that I was translating the epinician odes and dithyrambs of Bacchylides—which shut them up. It was as good as Auden's reply, in bar cars of railroad trains, when some hearty fellow passenger asked what he did: not wanting to say "poet," because that opened a can of very tired worms, he would reply, "medieval historian."

*   *   *

Bacchylides's work was known only by 107 nonsequential lines (in 69 fragments) until the discovery a century ago of a papyrus in Egypt with a text of Greek uncials which Sir Wallis Budge bought, cut up into sections, smuggled out of Egypt, and delivered to the British Museum in 1896. There Frederic Kenyon, an eminent papyrologist, reassembled 1382 lines, of which about 1070 were perfect or easily restored. It was his initial edition of twenty poems, six of them nearly complete, that was published in 1897.

The classical faculties being what they are, these poems became the property of Pindarists; they were, after all, in the same genre and from the same period. Not surprisingly, the Pindarists mostly had a vested interest in Pindar. As Ann Pipin Burnett shrewdly observes in her excellent study of Bacchylides, "If his unfamiliar epinicians in some detail resembled the well-known ones of his rival, it was always Bacchylides who was accused of imitation; but on the other hand, wherever his songs strove for their own effects, they were reproached for not living up to the mode and style of the great Theban master. Indeed, the students of Pindaric poetry almost succeeded in burying Bacchylides all over again, for their partisan criticism persuaded specialists in other realms that the newly found poet was 'like Pindar only worse,' and consequently many students of antiquity never made his acquaintance at all."[2]

It is also true that, to the modern reader, an epinician ode is at best a stretch. These are victory poems (epi-Niké-an) about sporting events! And there are stories of the gods and heroes woven into them, as compliments to the rich patron whose horses had won and from whom the poet was looking to be paid. They seem to us, at least at first blush, just a little extravagant, mannered displays of strenuous and elaborate toadying.

2. *The Art of Bacchylides* (Cambridge, Mass.: for Oberlin College by Harvard University Press, 1985).

Well, yes, in a way, they are. But if the poet can relate the patron and subject of these odes to the gods and heroes, it is a connection that works both ways, and it follows that, through the poetry, those grand and shadowy figures are inevitably revivified and refreshed. These poems, then, and the occasions they celebrate are the blood without which the disembodied spirits cannot speak. It is this doubleness that legitimates these pieces and makes them interesting and, to my mind, appealing.

What is required on the part of the poet is a kind of tact in order to effect this connection without looking silly. It is an exercise in nuanced modulation, a high-wire act in which the risks are great, and by the slightest misstep the poet may embarrass himself, his patron, and his art. When I alluded earlier to John Dryden, it was with a particular poem in mind, "To the Pious Memory of the Accomplished Young Lady Mrs. Anne Killigrew, Excellent in the Two Sister Arts of Poesie and Painting." This is one of the greatest poems in English. It is less well known than it ought to be, but as Alec D. Hope explains in his splendid discussion of the piece, "There is a skill in poetry which has an analogy with the technique of modulation in music. A long poem of any kind cannot be sustained indefinitely at the highest level and a poet's problem is to learn to maintain the tone of the poem as a whole, while modulating skillfully from one level to another. Now that long poems are rarely attempted it is not only an art which is in danger of being lost, but one which readers and critics often fail to recognize and appreciate."[3]

It is just that defect in readers and critics that has elevated Milton and Pindar (as if their sublimities needed any further elevation) at the expense of other poets with more delicate and various gifts. Bacchylides is quite capable of loftiness, but he can also venture an occasional folksiness or even displays of humor that seem to me authentic and agreeable signs of modesty and mental health. These are not Pindaric notes that Bacchylides sounds in his first ode:

Listen: you have your health
and enough to live on? What else can you want?
You're one of the lucky few
and ought to enjoy it.
Life, if you aren't sick or destitute,
is good, but we waste our time

3. In *The Cave and the Spring: Essays on Poetry* (Chicago: University of Chicago Press, 1965).

in this golden sunshine looking
always to someone else and thinking,
he must be happy.
It's not so.
The rich are never content.
They want, as fervently as we do,
more, more.
It's how men are made.
They want what they don't have,
whatever is hard to attain,
and they spend their strength
reaching out, mostly for baubles and toys,
wealth and power.

What is interesting is how he can then transform the tone abruptly. The passage to which he is leading us is altogether consonant with Pindar's solemnity, but it has its distinctive impact, I think, because of its surprise:

But these are trivial things,
and the bone yards are full
of utter non-entities
who had more than their share.

Areté is different, difficult, real:
those who have earned that have it forever,
in life and after, forever.
True distinction, fame, glory, *kleos*,
that never dies.

The vicissitudes of his literary fortunes would have amused Bacchylides, I am sure. His return from the land of shadows and the tepid reception he has found would have prompted, I should imagine, the contemplation of a number of myths that suggest themselves. The texture of that contemplation would have been rich and chewy, for he was realistic enough to understand what few of us are willing to admit—that luck plays a great part in what happens to us. Or call it, if you prefer, the favor of the gods. Because it is capricious and unreliable, we can never trust it; but this is the world that is, and one ignores it at his peril.

The text I have used is that of David A. Campbell in the Loeb Classical Library edition, *Greek Lyric*, vol. 4 (Cambridge, Mass.: Harvard University Press, 1992), with occasional glances at Fagles's and Burnett's versions.

EPINICIAN ODES

Ode I

Pierian Muses, daughters
of Zeus who rules
on high, you are famed for your
skill with the lyre: strum
and weave for us then intricate
songs for Argeius, the junior boxer,
the Isthmian games' victor.
The son-in-law of wise
Nereus, he is one from Ceos,
our own island, who
ventured as far away as
Corinth's god-built gates
to shine in that shining
Peloponnese island. . . . .

[4 lines missing]

. . . . yoked his horses to chariots,
and they flew across the meadows
of thick clouds, as if
in the sleep of maidens
these bore their dream cargo,
honey to the mind. Thus was established
our ancient city, here on the shores of the sea,
an ornament under the rays of
the golden sun. . . . .

[16 lines missing]

. . . . .with her sister, Makelo, loving
     the distaff,
by Elixus, that fair-flowing stream,
and Dexithea speaks
in submissive, welcoming voice
to two weary travelers, mighty Zeus
and his brother Poseidon,
and offers these disguised
strangers food and drink,
and after the meal addresses them.
I am, she says, bereaved with a double-edged
grief sharp as a Cretan ax . . . .

in deprivation altogether,
the two of us here . . . .

[30 lines missing]

On the third day after, the warlike
Minos came with his host of Cretans in fifty
ships, the bronze of their shields
flashing astern,
and he, by the will of Zeus,
dispenser of glory to men,
took that wasp-waisted girl,
Dexithea, the same
who had given the gods good welcome.
When King Minos departed
he left behind half his troop,
brave men, battle-loving,
to whom he gave this craggy island
as their portion, but he
sailed away to his fair city,
Knossos, that son of Europa
and mighty Zeus.

At the end of her term that raven-tressed
bride brought forth a boy-child,

a grandson of Zeus, Euxantius, the first
ruler over our splendid island,
here in our town that is washed
into loveliness in the evening sunlight. . .

[9 lines missing]

From Euxantius' line, descended
in time our Argeius, strong
of hand and mighty in spirit
as any lion, ready always
for battle. Light on his feet,
the son does not lack his father's
abundant virtues, those
Apollo, that brilliant archer,
bestowed on Pantheides:
the art of healing, and decent
respect toward guests. In his lifetime
he enjoyed the Graces' favor
and the admiration of many men.
And he left us as legacy
five much-praised sons, of whom
one Zeus from his seat on high
has made a victor at the Isthmian games,

in recompense for good deeds, his and his forebears'.
He has allotted a share
of the dazzling garlands.
I say it now and I always will,
for the truth does not change:
excellence, *areté*, has the greatest glory.
Wealth can consort with layabouts
and scoundrels, and flatter,
beguiling their thoughts;
but that man who excels before the gods
holds in his heart a more reliable,
better, and more glorious prospect.

    Listen: you have your health
and enough to live on? What else can you want?
You're one of the lucky few
and ought to enjoy it.
Life, if you aren't sick or destitute,
is good, but we waste our time
in this golden sunshine looking
always to someone else and thinking,
he must be happy.
It's not so.
The rich are never content.

They want, as fervently as we do,
more, more.
It's how men are made.
They want what they don't have,
whatever is hard to attain,
and they spend their strength
reaching out, mostly for baubles and toys,
wealth and power.
But these are trivial things,
and the bone yards are full
of utter non-entities
who had more than their share.
Areté is different, difficult, real:
those who have earned that have it forever,
in life and after, forever.
True distinction, fame, glory, *kleos*,
that never dies.

Ode II

Come Fame,
whose favor all men revere,
speed here to holy Ceos
bringing your grace
and the news that our Argeius won,
is victor in the battle of bold hands.

We think of the great achievements
of men of Euxantius' island,
winners at the famous
neck of the Isthmus,
of seventy garlands.

The Muse of our rocky coastline
summons the sweet drone of the reed flutes
to honor him, the dear son
of beloved Pantheides,
with the chanting of victory odes.

Ode III

The praises of fertile Sicily's
mistress, Demeter,
and of her daughter, Persephone,
adorned in purple, Clio,
giver of such sweet gifts,
sing in honor of Hieron's
fleet-footed horses.
How splendid they were at Olympia.
Niké, the goddess of victory,
blessed them, and Aglaia, goddess of glory,
smiled to see them run by that rushing
river, Alpheus, a babble of celebration.
Hail Deinomenes' son,
the winner of garlands.
To him the people shout,
"Oh thrice-blessed!"

Zeus has appointed him
to rule over many Greeks,
and he does not hide his
staggering wealth away
under night's mattress,
but temples are busy with traffic
of spotless cattle
for sacrifice; the streets
are crowded with strangers
secure in the laws of hospitality.
Gold is everywhere, a glitter
of finely wrought
tripods that flank the Delphic
temple's entrance where Phoebus
presides. The ability thus
to honor the god is the true
wealth, the spirit's mettle.
Consider Croesus, the ruler
of Lydia's horsemen,
when Zeus in the ripeness
of time made good his threat.
Sardis had fallen; the mighty
Persians had conquered. Croesus
had heaped wood on the pyre

within the palace walls, the means
of escape from the tears of enslavement
for him, his wife, and his daughters.
Together, they climbed to the platform,
and Croesus looked to the heavens and raised his fist:

"Zeus! What does this mean? What sense is there?
Where is the thanks of the gods? Where
is Lord Apollo? My father's house is in ruins.
Countless treasure I gave to Delphi.
But here are the savage Persians.
The Pactolis eddies crimson with Lydian blood.
Cyrus' lecherous soldiers
are dragging our women, hidden
in houses, into the broad streets.
That death men hate I have learned
to welcome as sweet." He ordered
his servants to set the pyre aflame.
And the daughters shrieked, and the wife
covered her eyes, for here was the death
mortals fear, and the flames crackled
beneath them. But Zeus sent thick black clouds
and a deluge to drench the fire. What
could Croesus think? Was he glad or angry

that what the gods do passes all understanding?
Apollo appeared and plucked them
up, him, his wife, and his delicate-ankled daughters
and whisked them away to the Hyperborean
lands, because he had been pious, generous,
giving the Pytho gifts of a richness
beyond those of any other mortal.

And of men who are living now
no one in all of Greece could dare claim
that he had sent to Apollo's shrine
at Delphi as much gold as you,
magnificent Hieron. Anyone
but those who gnaw the lean bone of envy
must praise a chivalrous man, warlike,
a lover of horseflesh,
who wields, moreover, the scepter
Zeus has assigned him.

I look for help to the Muses
with their blue-black hair,
to bless my song of how, in this life,
contingent, ephemeral,
a few things somehow endure.

Did not Apollo speak of this
to Admetus? "A mortal, you must live
in time, understanding that each day may be
your last, but knowing, too, that chances are
you will live for fifty years, and in peace
and plenty." A puzzle, the spirit's serene answer
to which is pious deeds. These are the truest
wealth. Those who are wise, know
what I am saying, as well as they know
how fresh air smells or water turns bluer,
almost black, offshore, or gold
is pleasing to touch and hold.
We all get old, turn gray,
and think of the days of our youth—
what bodies we had! But the worth of a man
does not diminish. The Muse preserves and nurtures
excellence. Hieron, whatever men can do,
you have done, and achievement requires more
than a reverent silence. We stroll in the public garden
of your good deeds, and our speaking of you
with gratitude and fondness, is a twittering of birds—
as of nightingales that used to sing
with their honey-sweet voices in faraway Ceos.

Ode IV

Golden-haired Apollo still loves
Syracuse and does honor to Hieron,
that city's upright ruler. Three times now
his praises are sung as a victor
at the Pythian games at that mountain ridge
close by the world's *omphalos*.
Let us all admire his fleet steeds!
Urania's sweet-voiced paraqueet,
I have performed before at the command
of that ruler of the lyre and with willing spirit
showered this champion with victory hymns.

In a just world with honest stewards,
this would be the fourth time
we would be doing Deinomenes' son
this ritual honor. Still, we may give him

this unique garland as the only man on earth
who can boast of this triple-crown in Cirrha's
vale by the glittering sea—
and that's not counting his two Olympian
triumphs. What can there be better
than to be thus loved by the gods
who grant you a generous share
of all kinds of blessings?

Ode V

Marshal of the men of Syracuse, those riders
of whirling horses, you are the man of the hour,
the man of destiny. Better than any alive
on the wide earth, you will understand rightly
this great honor, the sweet gift
of the violet-bedecked Muses.
Calm yourself, take solace from care,
and consider in your well-tempered mind
this hymn, woven with help of the slender Graces.
From the holy island Ceos your guest-friend,
Urania's clever servant sends
to your glorious city this song in praise
of Hieron, pouring out the voice of his heart.

High overhead, cleaving the currents of air
with his powerful wings, the golden eagle,

the Thunderer's messenger, minion of wide-ruling
Zeus, soars in his awesome strength,
and twittering birds flee in fear.
The mountain peaks of the earth
are nothing to him, nor the rough waves
of the ever-surging sea.
In the endless and empty sky,
he adjusts the pitch of his wings,
riding the powerful updrafts.
Down below, as men look up,
they feel in their hearts that grand soaring.

How should I begin? What chords
should my fingers strum? Thanks, first,
to Niké of the raven tresses and Ares
with his bright bronze breastplate
who has favored in battle the noble
sons of Deinomenes, you and your brothers.
May the god never tire of doing you good.
Beside the swirling Alpheus, golden Dawn
looked down to see Pherenicus' chestnut mane
and the victory of your horse,
running with the speed of an oncoming storm,
as she'd seen him win at the holy Pythian games.

Laying my hand on the sacred earth, I swear:
never in any race has he breathed the dust
of a faster horse. In the lead from start to finish,
he has the strength of a gale wind from the north
as he does what the jockey asks of him and more
on his way to new triumphs and new applause
for the great Hieron.
Fortunate is he to whom the gods
allot the finest things:
a rich life and a long one,
and good luck, for no man on this earth
is destined to have it all.

They say that the gate-wrecker,
Herakles, indomitable son
of Zeus of the lightning bolts, went down
to Hades, to Persephone's gloomy
halls to fetch back to the light
the sharp-fanged Cerberus, that offspring
of the snake, horrid Echidna.
There by the streams of Cocytus, he saw
the souls of forlorn mortals
swirled in the wind like leaves on Ida's headlands.
Among them, he spotted the ghost

of Meleager, that bold spear-wielding
grandson of old Porthaon.

When the hero, Alcmene's son, saw him
shining in armor, he stretched his taut
bowstring on his strong bow, opened
his quiver lid, and drew out
a bronze-tipped arrow. But Meleager's
ghost loomed up before him and spoke
as friend to friend: "Son of almighty Zeus,
steady there. Be calm. Your arrows
are useless against the dead. But you needn't
fear." And Herakles, astonished,
asked, "What god or mortal are you? In what
land did you live? Who killed you?
Jealous Hera who hates me will surely recruit
him to do me in, but that's for Athena
to deal with, as well as she can."

Meleager answered almost in tears, "It's hard
for mortals to sway the minds of the gods.
My father, horse-driving Oeneus,
tried to appease holy Artemis' anger.
He begged and sacrificed many white goats

and red-backed cattle. But the goddess, adamant,
sent a violent boar, a monstrous beast,
to Calydon's woods and fields
to rage like a flood, cut down grape vines,
savage the flocks, and even kill human beings,
whoever was bold enough or foolish enough
to venture outside the town.

    We came, then, the best of the Greeks,
to track him down and do battle against him,
hunted for six days and nights.
Luck or some god favored us, the Aetolians,
and we killed the boar, and buried
those of our number the tusker had gored
in its violence: Ancaeus and Agelaus, my brothers,
the best of the sons Althaea had born
in the halls of Oeneus' palace, world-famous and rich.

    But they weren't the only victims
of ruinous fate for Artemis, Leto's awesome
daughter, still held her grudge. The survivors
commenced to quarrel and then to fight
for the animal's blood-red hide, we on one side,

and the Curetes clan on the other.
Among those I killed were Iphiclus and the valiant
Aphares, my mother's nimble brothers.
When the blood is up, Ares recognizes
no friend in a brawl. Spears
and arrows fly every which way
from hands to the bodies and souls
of adversaries, dealing death
to whomever the god chooses.

That's how it was, but my angry mother,
Thestius' noble daughter, wouldn't buy it.
Enraged, she set herself to the business
of my destruction and took from its ornate
chest the log of my fate, that piece
of wood on which the Fates had said
my life depended, and threw it into the fire.
I happened to be, at that moment, just at the point
of slaying the brave Clymenus, Daïpylus' son,
who was built like a marble statue. I'd just caught up,
and we were in front of Pleuron's ancient towers.
The others had fled into that well-built city.
My soul shriveled; I knew my strength was gone.
Aaaaaarrrrghghgh.

In tears, I breathed my last
as I left behind my life in its splendid youth."

They say that was the only time that Herakles,
utterly fearless in battle, ever wept—
in pity for the fate of this man
and the grief he'd endured.
And he answered Meleagar,
saying : "It is the best thing
for mortals not to be born, never to see
the light of the sun. But there is no good
in lamenting. One must do one's best
in a terrible situation.
Is there, perhaps, in the house
of your brave father,
a daughter, a girl who looks
at all like you?
I would, in an instant, make her
my bride." And stalwart
Meleager's ghost managed
to make the reply:
"Back home I left a sister, Deianeira.
The skin on her neck is smooth
as a fresh olive. Of Aphrodite's sweet

blandishments, that girl has never heard
even the faintest whisper."

White-armed Calliope, stop right there.
Sing the praises of Zeus, the son of Cronus,
Olympus' ruler, and celebrate
the stream of Alpheus, untiring,
ever refreshed. Proclaim the strength
of Pelops, buried here,
and Olympia, where Pherenicus
ran his race, won his glorious victory,
and went back home
to Syracuse, that city of fine towers,
to bring Hieron the prize—the olive wreath.

In truth and for its sake, we
must learn to conquer envy,
push it away with both our hands
when any man does well, and offer our praises.
Hesiod, the Boeotian, faithful servant
of the Muses, put it this way:
"Him, whom the gods honor,
let men learn to honor also."
I am happy to send to Hieron my victory ode

which strays not at all from the narrow path
of truth. Such speech is the mulch
in which great trees of good fortune
may flourish. I pray that Zeus,
the great father may guard that grove
of blessings, and let them continue to grow
undisturbed in peace.

Ode VI

Lachon has brought home the bacon
or, say, the glory from almighty Zeus:
the first prize in the sprint. By Alpheus'
mouth, chalk up yet another Olympic
win for vine-rich Ceos, home of the greatest
boxers and runners,
who stand there as the anthem plays,
and feel the weight of those luxuriant
victory garlands they wear
on their high-held heads.
Now by the goddess Niké's will,
we sing, at the gate of your house,
Urania's hymn to honor
the son of Aristomenes,
fast as the wind.
Your triumph in this race
brings glory to Ceos.

Ode VII

A glorious day, the daughter of doting
parents, Time and Night,
the fifty months have dragged out between the games
and you have come at last.
Today, by the will of almighty
Zeus, the speed of foot and strength of bodies
among all Greeks will be judged.

The sixteenth day of the month, to you
it is given to hand out prizes and honors
to those few envied men
whom the god of victory has blessed.
You are Lachon's, Aristomenes' son,
as he is yours.

. . . Chaerolas, his ancestor,

. . . . death . . . . native land. . . . .

. . . . decided to . . . .

. . . . childless

Ode VIII

. . . . . vine rich . . . horseless [Ceos?] . . . .
. . . . of the contest . . . .
. . . .
. . . . .singing the
    praises of Pytho
where sheep are slaughtered,
and Nemea, and the Isthmus,
and I will make my boast,
swearing and laying my hand
on the sacred earth,
that every payment of my praise
has the ring of authentic truth—
no Greek, boy or man, has ever won
more victories in his class.
Zeus, whose spear
is the lightning bolt in the sky

by the turbid banks of Alpheus,
may you, too, grant his prayers
for glory, and place on his head
a wreath of gray-green olive
from Aetolian trees
in the famous athletic contests
of Phrygian Pelops.

Ode IX

You, the Graces with your golden
distaffs, your gift of fame inspires
the minds of men.
Mouthpiece of the sloe-eyed Muses,
I am about to sing the praises of Phlius
and the rich plain of Nemean Zeus,
where pale-armed Hera reared
the sheep-slaughtering roaring lion,
as the first of Herakles' far-renowned labors.

    There the best of the Argives, those heroes
with crimson shields, the troops Adrastus led
on their way to Thebes, held their games
for the first time in honor of Nemea's
prince, Archemorus, whose name betokens
"the beginning of fate." That dismal promise

fulfilled itself when a fiery-eyed
viper, huge, appeared and bit him,
killed him while he slept:
a sign, an omen of slaughter to come.
Ah, implacable fate!
Amphiarius, Oicles' son, tried
but could not persuade them
to return to the streets thronged with valiant
fighters. Hope can drive men mad,
as here, for she sent Adrastus to Thebes
to fight in support of the claim
of horse-breaking Polyneices.
That kind of fame attaches still
to athletes who crown their hair with garlands
from Nemea's glorious contests
every odd-numbered year. Theirs
is true eminence. And now a god
has awarded Automedes the victory
for how he shone among the pentathletes
as the full moon does in the mid-month's
clear night sky and blots out
all the stars. Before the crowds
of cheering Greeks, he showed what a body
can do, hurling the discus, or heaving

the javelin shaft from his hand
high through the sky. He performed
the nimble wrestling holds,
and pinned strong-limbed bodies to earth
with spirit and strength. Then he returned
to Phlius' swirling waters of the Asopus
River, the fame of which has flowed
to every land, even the Nile's headwaters
where Memnon ruled. And the Amazons,
those strange, spear-carrying ladies
who live by Thermodon's banks,
the daughters of Ares, met
Asopus' descendants, Telamon
and Peleus, with whom they did
hard battle, and at high-gated Troy,
the Scamander saw
what Telemon's son and Peleus'
accomplished. Through the histories of men
one sees the footprints of Asopus' offspring
treading their intricate paths
everywhere. His daughters were
dark-haired Thebe and lovely Aegina,
whom great Zeus took to bed
and who bore the hero Aeacus . . . .

To these, his children,
the gods gave good fortune, as founders
of prosperous cities that never would be sacked.
. . . . . . .who of the land of the Achaeans
. . . . trials . . . .
. . . . .with beautiful robe. . . . . .
. . . .
. . . . . . .and Corinth's fountain, Peirene,
with twisted garlands, and other notable daughters
of the ancient and resounding river
who were overcome in the beds of glorious gods.
. . . . .city . . . .
. . . . .victory . . . .
. . . . the skirl of flutes . .

. . . . to praise, too, the sun-tanned,
violet-haired Cypris, the glorious
mother of Passions, well known to all mortals

. . . . a hymn that. . . . .

. . . . .even when you have died . . . .

. . . . everlasting ages,
would tell the ensuing generations

of your victory at Nemea: a splendid deed deserving
songs of honest praise that is stored up on high
with the gods, and that men remember.
This, the Muses' finest adornment, is what we leave
even after death. There are many paths for men;
but the mind of the gods sees what is hidden
in the dark of night
. . . . and the better man
. . . . to a few men the gift of foresight
of what will be.
. . . . gave . . . .
. . . . grace . . . .
. . . . and Dionysus' city, honored by the gods
to dwell . . . .
. . . . golden-sceptered . . . .
. . . . whoever takes
a fine thing . . . .
praise him: for the son of Timoxenos,
with processions of the young men,
sing praises for his victory in the pentathlon.

Ode X

Fame, you visit the nations of men, and . . . . .
. . . . eyes. . . . .
peaceful respite. . . . .
now for him his brother-in-law has prompted
yours truly, the island's bumble bee
to produce this honeyed buzz of approbation.
An artifact, you want, of the deathless Muses
for all men of culture and learning
to have at hand and enjoy.
Thus may your excellence be revealed
everywhere on earth . . . .
with Niké's blessing, you have won
the garland of blossoms for your fair head
and brought glory to Athens
and fame to the clan of Oeneidae,
for in Poseidon's games, famous

throughout the world, you showed
all Greeks the blur of your swift feet.

    I sing, then, of how he reached the finish line,
gasping out gusts of hot breath, and again
how he wet the crowd's clothes with droplets
of olive oil, as he sped past
the close-packed grandstand at the fourth turn.
The herald of the stewards twice
proclaimed him an Isthmian victor.
Twice, at Nemea, also,
near Zeus' sacred altar, he was a winner.
Glorious Thebes gave him a hero's welcome
and at wide Argos and at Sicyon
there were parades and many lusty cheers
from those who dwell in Pellene
and rich Euboea and on Aegina,
that holy island. Each man seeks a different
road to glory; and the different kinds
of knowledge among mankind are beyond
counting. Skill at some art or craft
can earn a man honor from the Graces.
Some rely on that. Others,
who prophecy, can look to that gift

as their hope. We all tread different
paths—in the archer's field or the herdsman's
meadow—but all to the same end,
which is the future where Fortune
waits to tip the scales this way
or that. But what finer ambition
can anyone have in his heart
than to be acclaimed by cheering crowds
and maybe even envied
as one who is truly noble?
There's nothing wrong with wealth,
but anyone can have large sums of money.
That's beside the point, which ought to be
uppermost in my mind,
and in all our minds: the triumph
and its delicious celebration, the massed
pipes resounding . . . .
 . . . . blending . . . .
 . . . . one must . . . .

Ode XI

Niké, giver of sweets, on you
has the father on high
atop golden Olympus, bestowed
great honor. Standing at Zeus'
elbow, you judge the achievement of *areté*,
acts of prowess for both mortals
and immortals. O daughter
of thick-haired and judicious Styx,
be gracious. Because of you,
Metapontion, the city honored by gods,
is filled even now with celebration,
and triumphal marches of handsome
and fit young men who sing
the Pythian victor's praises,
Alexidamus, the splendid son
of Phaiscus. Apollo, whom Leto bore
in Delos, received him with a kindly eye;

because of how he wrestled
with matchless strength, garlands
fell in profusion around him
at the Pythian games on Cirrha's plain.
The sun never, on that grand day,
saw him fall. And I tell you that, two years ago,
at Olympia near Alpheus' lovely
stream in the precinct sacred to holy Pelops,
if justice had not been perverted, the olive wreath
for which all compete there, too,
would have crowned his head
as he returned to his homeland,
cattle-breeding Italy,
for in the land of lovely choruses,
he brought one young man after another
to earth, by his strength and his nimble wits.
But because of a god or the errant judgment of men
the highest honor there was snatched
from his hands. But now Artemis
of the woods with her golden distaff,
the Gentle One, the famous archer,
has awarded him this dazzling victory.

    To her once, Proetus, Abas' son,
the king of Tiryns set up an altar,

where many prayers would be offered,
he and his beautifully-robed daughters,
whom mighty Hera had driven out
of their grand palace in fear,
yoking their minds to a violent obsession:
maidens still, they entered the sanctuary
of the purple-belted goddess to boast
that their father was richer by far
than holy Zeus' consort.
In a snit, then she put a crazy thought
into their heads, and they scurried off
to the woods and the mountainsides,
uttering high shrill screams,
strangers now to civilization, cities,
Tiryns and its familiar god-built streets.
This was the tenth year
since the bronze-armored heroes,
fearless in battle, and their much-envied
king had left Argos, the city loved
by gods, and lived in Tiryns.
An insurmountable strife between the brothers,
Proetus and Acrisius, had grown up
from a trivial start. With outrageous
feuding and grievous battles,
they were ruining their people,

who, in desperation, begged the sons
of Abas, with that land so rich in barley,
that the younger of the two should be permitted
to found a city in Tiryns,
before they were all destroyed.
And Zeus son of Cronus, honored
his blood-kin, Danaus,
and his nephew and son-in-law,
the horse-driving Lynceus.
And the god was willing
to relieve their hateful troubles.
So the mighty Cyclopes came,
and labored hard to build
a magnificent wall for the radiant
city, where the godlike heroes lived,
having left behind them horse-pasturing
Argos. From this Tiryns it was
that the dark-haired daughters of Proetus
rushed in their wild flight. And woe
overcame Proetus' heart, and the eerie thought
struck him—that he would plant
his double-edged sword deep in his chest.
But his loyal spearmen restrained him,
with gentling words and the force

of their strong hands. For a year and a month,
his daughters roamed and wandered
like wild beasts in the forest's shadows
and fled through the sheep-nourishing fields
of Arcadia's hills. When their father came
at last to Lusus' stream, he washed himself
in its water and called on Leto's daughter,
Artemis, who wears the crimson headdress.
Imploring the ox-eyed goddess, he stretched
his hands to the sun's rays and asked
that she deliver his poor daughters
from the grip of their dreadful madness.
"I will sacrifice to you twenty red-backed oxen,
never yoked," he said. And the huntress goddess,
hearing his prayer, interceded with Hera,
who relieved the god-forsaken girls
of their madness. In thanks for this
they built her a sanctuary and an altar
they stained red with the blood of sheep,
and they founded a women's chorus
to chant never-ending prayers.

From there you accompanied the brave
Achaean men to Metapontion,

their horse-nurturing city;
where, fortunate, you dwell, the people's
mistress. A lovely grove near Casas'
limpid waters they dedicated to you,
when in the fullness of time,
by the will of the blessed gods, they sacked
with the bronze-armored sons of Atreus,
Priam's far-off well-built city
at Troy. Any fair-minded judge
would have to admit the proposition
that, throughout time, there have been
deeds of valor, more than a man can number,
done by the stalwart Achaeans.

Ode XII

Like a skillful pilot, Clio,
mistress of song, guide my mind aright
if you ever did. For queenly Niké
commands me to the prosperous island of Aegina,
to my hospitable friends, to adorn
their god-built city, singing
of the strong-limbed wrestling at Nemea . . . .

[24 lines missing]

. . . . in the regional games,
and for thirty splendid victories
they were honored with celebrations,
some in Pytho, others at the isthmus
of Pelops' pine-covered holy island,
and still others in the Nemean grove

of Zeus, the god of shining lightning bolts . . . .
these triumphs . . . .
and beside the bright-swirling [of Alpheus?] . . . .

[27 lines missing]

Ode XIII

[8 lines missing]

. . . . .Clio . . . .

[34 lines missing]

". . . . . He [Herakles] shall prevent
    them
from vain violence, handing down judgments
of law for mortals: look how Perseus'
great-grandson brings down his hand
like a cudgel on the neck
of the savage lion with strength but
deftness, too! For the gleaming,
man-killing bronze
just won't pierce the lion's

awesome body;
the sword bends back.
I prophesy that someday there will be
sweaty work for Greeks here,
when they compete
for garlands in the pancration."
Now, beside the altar of Zeus,
the mightiest ruler, the garlands of
glory-bringing Niké nurture
dazzling fame for men
throughout their lives—anyway, for a few—and
when the gloomy cloud of death
covers them over, the everlasting *kleos*
of their fine deed is left behind,
immutable and secure.

And you, too, Pytheas, son of Lampon,
have achieved this at Nemea; your hair
is crowned with garlands of perfect blossoms,
as you walk the grand streets of Aegina
and your ancestral island swarms
with the victory processions, in which we mortals
take delight and strength, celebrating
your overpowering strength in the pancration.

Gentle Aegina, daughter of Asopus,
who is lord of the swirling river, Zeus gives you
a great honor that blazes among all Greeks,
a bright flambeau. Somewhere a maiden sings
your praises and dances in your honor, bounding
like a playful fawn on the flowery meadow
with her noble attendants,
their hair adorned with garlands of bright red flowers.
They sing of your son, Aeacus, and celebrate
the lovely Endaïs who bore him the godlike
Peleus and the valiant Telamon.

I raise my voice to proclaim their children's
    glory—
the fleet Achilles, and the Ajax,
the spirited son of gorgeous Eriboea,
that shield-bearing hero who stood there
at his ship's stern and stopped the courageous
Hector who rushed down the beach, his helmet
    plumes
aquiver, to torch the Achaean ships.
This was when Achilles, in his great wrath,
had withdrawn from the fighting,
a menace no longer. Until then,

the Trojans had cowered beyond their walls
all but paralyzed in their terror of battle
with fierce Achilles, who had raged across the plain
brandishing over his head his much-bloodied
spear. But he withdrew from the fighting,
that fearless son of Thetis. Think of a gale
on the darkly billowing sea that frightens
the sailors, tossing their boat this way
and that. But then, at the break of dawn,
it gentles, and, as the light comes up,
the water smoothes itself, and the men
take heart and reset their sails
for the light wind now that will take them
back to dry land they had given up all hope
of ever seeing again. In just that way,
when the Trojans heard that Achilles now skulked
in his tent because of the lovely Briseïs, they turned
to the gods, raising their arms in thanks and praise,
as if they were mariners seeing that dawn
breaking and the storm at last subsiding.
Quickly they streamed from Laomedon's
walls, swarming onto the plain to do valiant
violent battle, and now it was
Greeks who were filled with fear.

Ares, lord of the spear, urged them on,
and Apollo, the Lycians' patron.
And the Trojans came to the seashore and fought
beside the high-pooped ships, and the dark shingle
ran red with the blood of men Hector had killed,
for he was the best, throughout this onslaught
of the Trojans' godlike heroes
in whose hearts he kindled fresh hopes.
With arrogant shouts, the Trojan horsemen
charged the dark-eyed ships to turn them away
and send them homeward again so their god-built
city would have dancing and feasts
to celebrate their salvation.
But they were doomed nonetheless
to die and to dye the whirling
Scamander crimson with their blood,
at the hands of the tower-destroying
Achilles and Ajax.

All these brave men are dead
and their bodies were burned on pyres
piled high with wood or buried
in earth, but their all-shining *areté*
can never be obscured or effaced

by the dark of night. For always in glorious *kleos*
that goddess roams the earth and the billowing seas
and properly honors Aeacus' fame-nurturing
island and guides the state with Renown and Order,
to whom we all give thanks in our festivals
for guarding the cities of pious men
and keeping the peace.

    Rejoice and sing, young men, of the glorious
win of Pytheas, and the care of skillful
Menander, his trainer and coach who came
from Athens and Alpheus' sacred stream.
Him majestic Athena has honored,
who has crowned the heads of countless athletes
with garlands in the panhellenic contests.

    Let anyone whom Envy has not struck dumb
praise these men, as is right and proper.
People find fault with anything we may do,
but the quibbles never last, and in time
the truth prevails to recognize
what has been well done,
and no one remembers the critics'
empty words . . . .

[10 lines missing]

. . . . .warms the heart
with new hopes. With such high expectations,
I too, trusting in the Muses
with their elegant headgear, present this tiara
of song to honor the lavish welcome
Lampon gave me. My praise of your fine son
I intend to be every bit as lavish.
Clio herself has refined this
melic offering of mine. These words,
if they delight, may spread
throughout the world and endure
broadcasting his name to all the people.

Ode XIV

To have a portion of good things from the gods
is man's best hope, but Fortune
can destroy even the great, if she comes
with a heavy enough burden.
As quickly can she raise any worthless person,
whenever she wants, to let him shine and dazzle.
Different ideas men have
of excellence and of honor, but one stands out
among them all: when a person tries to do
right, attending to what is at hand and gives
his best. In the pains of battle and moments
of deep sorrow, the lyre's strings should be stilled,
and the voices of men in their clear-sounding chorus
ought to be mute. No clangor
of cymbal, then, or ruffle of festive
drum: for every event in the lives of men,

there are proper forms of behavior.

When someone does well, by the grace of a god,

we must sing our declarations of thanks

and praise—as to Cleoptolemus now,

the glorious son of Pyrrichus we celebrate.

This child of a just and generous man,

at Poseidon's Petraean games,

won with his horses . . . .

DITHYRAMBS

Dithyramb I

The slender Theano, the wife
of godlike Antenor, battle-rousing
Athena's priestess
[opened the] golden [doors of the temple?] . . . .

. . . . of the Argives, to Odysseus,
Laertes' son,
and Menelaus, Atreus' royal son,
and spoke . . . .

. . . . well-built . . . . with the gods

[9 lines missing]

. . . . heart, ... at midnight

[13 lines missing]

[Antenor's sons] led [the envoys in]
and their father, the hero of good counsel, relayed
to King Priam and his sons all
those things the Achaeans had said.
Forthwith, the heralds
made haste through the broad streets
of the city and brought out the Trojans
of all ranks and degrees into the great
agora where the army assembles.
Rumor ran, as it always does,
rife, and raising their hands to the deathless
gods the people prayed for an end to their troubles.

Say, then, Muse, who was the first to begin
the righteous pleading? Menelaus, son
of Pleisthenes, spoke
with beguiling words in a resonant
voice, having been coached by the splendidly robed
Graces: "Bellicose Trojans, Zeus,
the ruler on high who sees all things,
is not to blame for the great anguish of mortals.
Every man has it within his power
to emulate unswerving Justice,
who keeps the door to the hall of the holy Eunomia

and prudent Themis, goddesses of good order.
Those who dwell with Justice thrive
and their children prosper.
But Hybris, that shameless one, tempts us all
with false hopes and lets us imagine
that greed and shiftiness are enough,
and with fast talk and a lot of nerve,
we can somehow get by. Those who believe her
look for the easy way,
supposing that somebody else's wealth
and power is theirs for the taking.
It never works, and she brings them,
sooner or later, to ruin, as she did
to those sons of the Earth,
the arrogant Giants."

Dithyramb II

. . . . and since Urania
from her lovely throne has sent me
a golden nef from Pieria
laden with these splendid songs . . . .
. . . . by the flowery Hebrus he takes
delight in [game?], or in a long-necked swan . . . . .
delighting his soul, ...
. . . . .you come, Pythian Apollo, to seek
the flowers of paeans the Delphic chorus
intones at your glorious temple.

Meanwhile we sing of Herakles: how
Amphitryon's brave-hearted son, left
Oechalia a ruin, destroyed by fire,
and arrived at the Euboean headland,
Cenaeum's promontory, with waves

breaking on all sides. There
would he sacrifice from the loot
of Eurytus' sacked city:
nine loud-bellowing bulls for mighty Zeus,
lord of the endless clouds, and two for Poseidon,
who rouses the sea to subdue the dry land,
and a high-horned ox, never yoked,
for the virgin Athena whose eyes blaze with power.

But then, Fate, a god no one can fight,
contrived for Deianeira, to her great grief,
a shrewd scheme. She heard the bitter
rumor: her husband, Herakles,
begotten by Zeus and utterly fearless
in battle, was sending home
to be his captive and no doubt concubine
the fair Iole, Eurytus' daughter.
Poor Deianeira! What was she to do?
Devastated by envy and blinded
by the ignorance of the future that is our lot,
she remembered Nessus' shirt, that gift
with a charm of great power—but not
what she was expecting.

Dithyramb III

A ship with a blue-black prow
cut through the Cretan sea. On board,
were steadfast Theseus, stalwart in battle,
and seven Ionian youths and seven maidens.
Bellying the iridescent sail,
a north wind blew, by Athena's will.

      The heart of the Cretan king Minos,
was inflamed by Aphrodite's abrupt attentions
and he could not keep his hands
from the white-cheeked maiden,
Eriboea. Afraid, the girl cried out
to Pandion's descendant, the brazen-armored
Theseus, who rolled his black eyes
beneath his beetling brows.
Sympathy tore at his vitals and he said:

"Son of almighty Zeus, the spirit
guiding your conduct is no longer pious.
Minos, take hold of yourself.
Whatever fate and the gods may have granted us,
and however the scales of Justice incline,
we shall, when the time comes, fulfill
our appointed destiny. Until then, I say to you,
desist from this outrageous behavior.
Io, the daughter of Phoenix, took Zeus to her bed
beneath the brow of Ida and gave birth to you,
great among mortals. That's true, but it's also true
that I was borne to Aethra, Pittheus' daughter
whom the sea god Poseidon had bedded
and to whom the Nereids gave that golden veil.
We are both the sons of gods, then, war lord of
        Knossos,
and I bid you cease and desist. Restrain yourself
from what you intend.
If you assault one of these youngsters
or force yourself on one of them, the dawn
and its lovely light is something you'll hate to see,
for that will be the day that you and I
will try the force of our arms and let the gods
decide between us."

So spoke the noble spear-wielding hero,
whose sailors were stunned at his boldness.
Minos, the son-in-law of the sun, was angry,
deeply angry, and contrived another plan.
"Mighty father Zeus," he said, "hear me!
If indeed that Phoenician girl bore me
as your true begotten son, send forth, I pray,
a fire-haired lightning bolt from the sky. Give me
a sign, unambiguous, splendid." Then he turned
to Theseus and said, "You claim that Aethra
bore you to the earth-shaking god Poseidon.
If so, you can bring this ornament on my hand
back from the ocean's depths, plunging down
to your father's home to retrieve my golden bauble.
We'll see if your prayers are answered or my own
are heard by the son of Cronus, the thundering god."

Zeus, the almighty, heard his blameless prayer,
and produced for Minos, who'd asked for it,
that majestic display of lightning bolts in the sky
for all to see, for the sake of the son he loved.
The warrior king, valiant in battle, looked up,
and his heart was warmed, and he stretched out
his hands to the heavens, saying,
"Theseus, look! Behold the gifts

of my father, Zeus. It is your turn now to leap
into the boisterous sea. We'll see
if your father, lord Poseidon, the son of Cronus,
will grant you a special glory throughout the verdant
earth." Thus he spoke. And Theseus' spirit
did not shrink; he stood on the well-built ship's
thwart and leapt, and the zone of the sea received
    him,
welcoming warmly. Zeus' son was astonished,
and he ordered the ornate vessel be held
headed into the wind; but Fate had set
another tack and bearing.
The fleet craft hurtled ahead, running
before a freshened north wind that drove it along.
The Athenian youths and maidens, filled with fear,
had watched the hero jump into the sea,
and they wept copious tears from their lovely eyes,
awaiting confirmation that he had drowned.
But dolphins that frisk and play in the sea had
    appeared
to escort the son to the home of his great father,
the lord of horses. To the hall of the august god,
Theseus came, and he saw Nereus' daughters,
beautiful to behold, and he was afraid,
for their splendid limbs dazzled as if on fire,

and bright ribbons of gold whirled in their hair
as they danced in their joy, their nimble feet
an amazement. And he saw in that splendid dwelling
Amphitrite, the holy, ox-eyed wife
of his godly father, who threw around his shoulders
a purple cloak and placed on his head a perfect
garland dark with roses, which Aphrodite
had brought as a wedding gift.

     Nothing the gods decree
is beyond the belief of reasonable men.
When Theseus reappeared beside the ship
at its tapered stern, Minos looked down and saw him,
and thought . . . What? What could he think?
He beheld, emerging out of the ocean
without a drop of water anywhere on him,
Theseus, shining with the grace of the gods
over his whole body.
The seven Athenian maidens sang a hymn
of thanks and praise.

                        Apollo, god of Delos,
may the songs we sing here in Ceos warm your heart.
Grant us your precious favors of peace and good
      fortune.

Dithyramb IV:
The Return of Theseus

Chorus

King of blessed Athens, lord
of the cosseted Ionians, why
does the bronze-belled trumpet now sound
its war song? Is there some enemy chieftain
raiding our borders? Do robbers plan
their wickedness against our shepherds,
the rustling of their flocks? What grief
tears at your heart? Tell, for I believe
that of all mortals you,
son of Pandion and Creusa,
can rouse the valiant warriors to battle.

Aegeus

A herald has just arrived, having run
all the way from the Isthmus. He tells
the all but untellable deeds of a mighty
man who has killed the terrible Sinis,
strongest of mortals, son of Lytaeus (he
was Poseidon's son). This Sinis liked to tie
his victims to bent pine trees he then released
to watch them get torn apart.
He has also slain
the man-killing boar in the Cremmyon valleys,
and vicious Sciron, the robber,
who threw men down from a cliff.
He has closed forever Cercyon's wrestling school,
where the master killed the losers, and taken the
    measure
at last of cruel Procrustes.
He has dropped the hammer
of his powerful father, Polypemon.
I fear how this will end.

Chorus

Who is the man? Where is he from? How
is he equipped? Does he lead an army
with materiel for war? Or is he alone
with only a few attendants,
a wayfarer like any other who wanders
in foreign lands, this strong man who is fearless
and has overpowered such notorious villains?
He must have the help of some god,
bringing justice this way on those who are wicked.
How else could he accomplish deed after deed,
surviving every trial?
And yet, in the course of time
all things come to an end.

Aegeus

The herald tells me
only two men are with him.
He has a sword
with an ivory hilt slung over his shoulder
and carries a pair of javelins in his hands.

On the fire-red hair of his head,
he sports a Laconian topee, and his tunic
of bright purple stuff covers his chest.
Over that is a woolen Thessalian cloak.
With eyes bright as the crater of Lemnos' volcano,
he is a boy in the prime of his youth,
who loves all Ares' toys and their clashing of bronze
against bronze in battle.
He is on his way here
and approaches splendid Athens.

Dithyramb V

There are countless tricks and tropes,
all manner of styles and modes of divine song
for one who has the Pierian Muses' gifts
and upon whose songs those sloe-eyed
maidens, the Graces, confer
a measure of honor.
Now, with the talent of famous Ceos,
let me make something new, here
in rich and beautiful Athens.
It is no mere local knack,
but one fit to travel the wide world,
for the genius of that place is blessed,
enriched by Calliope's generous help.

There was a time, once, when the peerless
heifer, Io, Inachus' daughter,

hurried from Argos, land of horses.
Mighty Zeus had told her to flee.
Golden-robed Hera, the queen of heaven,
bade Argus keep his hundred eyes
open and always upon her,
to guard the beautiful beast.

Hermes, Maia's son, could not get past him,
in bright daylight or in darkness of holy night.
What happened then? Did Zeus' messenger kill . . . . ?
Or was it that . . . .
with powerful offspring . . . . Argus?
. . . . unutterable cares?
Or did
the Pierian Muses bring about . . . .
. . . . rest from troubles . . . . ?

For me, the safest path is the one
that leads me to the end, when she arrived
at the Nile's flowery banks. [Gadfly-driven?]
Io bore [in her womb?] the child [of Zeus?],
Epaphus. There [she gave birth to him?],
the ruler over linen-robed [Egyptians?]
teeming with majestic . . . .

and greatest . . . . among mortals

. . . . from this race Cadmus, son of

    Agenor,

sired Semele in seven-gated Thebes,

and she bore Dionysus, who inspires

Bacchantes . . . . choirs.